PRAIRIE KADDISH

ארקטישער אָקעאַן

אַלאַסקע

ווערמאָנירע
אינזלען

פאראייניגטע טעריטאָריע

יוקאָן

קאָלאָמביער לאַנד

אבצ

אַלבבערטאַ סאַסקאַ-
טשעוואַן

בריטיש
קאַלאָמביע קאַנאַדע

עדמאָנטאָן

רעגינע

וואַנקאָווער חיקטאָריע

וואַשינגטאָן

ארעגאָן

קאַליפאָרניע

נעוואַדאַ

מאָנטאַנאַ

אַרעגאָן

פאראייניגטע שטאַאַטען

Prairie Kaddish

ISA MILMAN

COTEAU
BOOKS

Edited by Don McKay.
Book and cover design by Duncan Campbell.
Cover image: "Woman in Field," by Kamil Vojnar / Photonica Collection, Getty Images.

Mixed Sources
Product group from well-managed forests and recycled wood or fiber
www.fsc.org Cert no. SGS-COC-2624
© 1996 Forest Stewardship Council

Printed and bound in Canada at Gauvin Press. FSC
The inside pages of this book are printed on recycled paper, 100% post-consumer fibers.

CIP data available at: *www.coteaubooks.com/bookpages/PrairieKaddish.html*

10 9 8 7 6 5 4 3 2 1

COTEAU
BOOKS

2517 Victoria Ave.
Regina, Saskatchewan
Canada S4P 0T2

AVAILABLE IN CANADA & THE US FROM
Fitzhenry & Whiteside
195 Allstate Parkway
Markham, ON, Canada, L3R 4T8

The publisher gratefully acknowledges the financial assistance of the Saskatchewan Arts Board, the Canada Council for the Arts, the Government of Canada through the Book Publishing Industry Development Program (BPIDP), Association for the Export of Canadian Books, and the City of Regina Arts Commission, for its publishing program.

Canada Council
for the Arts

Conseil des Arts
du Canada

SASKATCHEWAN
ARTS BOARD

Canada

CITY OF REGINA

ז"ל

Sabina Kramer Milman

. . . and it is something like that,
some feeling in the arrest of the image
that what perishes and what lasts forever
have been brought into conjunction.
— ROBERT HASS

my soul lies in the dust; by your word revive me.
— PSALM 119 (ד) (25)

CONTENTS

STEPPING THROUGH THE GATE

*T*his is a book of mourning and celebration. A book of history in poetic form. It is also an accidental book that began as I prepared for the Sage Hill writer's retreat, at St. Michael's monastery near Regina. A friend suggested that I visit the Lipton Hebrew Cemetery, not far away, where some of her ancestors were buried. I had lived nearly thirty years in Canada, and never knew that Jews had come to Saskatchewan as pioneer settlers, a century before. Stunned by my ignorance, I was determined to visit that cemetery. Although I felt an urgency about it, I was completely unaware that my life was about to change, that a chance suggestion would lead me on a prairie pilgrimage through the fields and towns of Saskatchewan, and then back in time, roughly 150 years, to the Europe my family came from.

Between 1880 and the First World War, one in three Jews left Eastern Europe to escape persecution and live free lives. My parents' parents were those who'd stayed behind. Every new world Jew had relatives back home. They were those relatives. My parents were among the lucky few who survived and came to North America a half century later. I had no idea that stepping through the gate of the Lipton Hebrew Cemetery would open for me an understanding and respect for how death is honoured in Jewish experience, and illuminate my place in the exquisite history of Jewish suffering and regeneration. From a region and time that had no register for me, I found where and how I belonged. But such is the way of discoveries – they usually happen when we are looking for something else.

Writing this book has brought me in contact with many people: some are elderly, some who have since died, and some that I've met through remarkable documents that I've come across – cherished photographs, letters, postcards, maps, reports and books. I've tried my best to bring them to life with the eloquence they deserve, while recognizing and honouring the ever so faint, but still active languages of Yiddish and Michif. The glossary beginning at page 111 explains all the foreign words and expressions. The Notes that follow indicate sources and may help readers unfamiliar with Yiddish prairie history.

So why use poetic form to tell this story? Poetry is song and chant that aligns the beat of mind and heart. It boils down the raw into an essence – a few choice words, arranged just so – and takes you to the soul place, our human home. In Hebrew, poetry and song are the same word. In Hebrew, *Kaddish,* the prayer for the dead, derives from *kadosh,* meaning holy. I'm not a religious person, but I do believe that we humans are all souls that are sacred. As a Jew, I believe that remembrance is in itself sacred. Without remembrance, we would not exist. With this work, I honour the souls of our ancestors, so many of whom have no one to remember them.

I'm chanting the prayer of remembrance.

My Prairie Kaddish.

Lipton Hebrew Cemetery. First Visit

After a hundred kilometres, past Cuper and Dysart, we saw the
mural on the old hotel, a *mogen david* hung in the painted sky,
a Jew in prayer-garb beneath, so unexpected it caught my breath,
across from the grain elevator by the railroad tracks, where the
road paralleled straight out of town. We'd never have found it if
we hadn't asked, stopping at the big barn where the garage sale
goes from Sunday through Sunday. They were used to strangers
stopping for directions to the cemetery, they said. In thanks
I bought a laser picture of the Last Supper, for a buck, because
Jesus and the Disciples looked very sweet, and it cheered me
to feel good about Jesus, and I wanted a souvenir
(I'm looking at it now).

Soon, a signpost, then white metal fence:

LIPTON HEBREW CEMETARY

higgledy piggledy little grave-houses built of brick and wood,
and whoa, *khaloshesdike* corrugated tin roofs,
rust stains bleeding down their slopes
(these are the graves?)
prairie grass prickled our feet, our view,
not a single tree,
no tended lawns,
not even a pebble
to mark a visit.

Why did they bury them that way?

Semblance of rows, men over here, women there, children scattered

Clara Ethel Sanfor   Kruger Children
a child of three years   Golda Dina Minnie

hayeled Mendel, (the boy) by the fence

Mrs. W, buried in the furthest northwest corner, all alone,
her house so disheveled, rotten wood giving way,
you can see right in, but there's nothing to see, in that darkness
(a kharpe un a bushe – a disgrace, I hear my mother say)

committed suicide 1918
(Me darf hobn rakhmones)   (a little pity please)

(The loose-leaf binder from the sweltering hut we took to
the air-conditioned car to read)

"she was despondent, slashed her throat
with butcher knife while husband abroad"

"her husband away for long periods
the winters so long and cold"

(at least they buried her within the gates)

LIPTON CEMETARY

Grave House

I stood in the old cemetery, shaken up and startled. Grave houses for Jewish burial? Was this a Romanian Jewish custom? Some were from Romania, others from Russia, and Russia, huge as it was, was more familiar, from my parents' stories of the old country. As far as I knew, there were no such grave houses there.

Jewish burial practice, like everything in Jewish life, was codified and regulated by two millennia of rabbis who ruled on the minutiae – down to the cleaning under the finger and toenails, and with the appropriate tool. I figured that grave houses were not in the rabbis' lexicon, or I would have seen them before.

So how do Jews usually take care of their dead? With a *khevra kadisha,* a holy burial society composed of volunteers who come, day or night, when called upon. Even in Lipton, where the Jewish settlers were spread around many miles of homesteading sections, they took care of everything: brought the wooden litter to carry the *mes* to the *besoylem,* where they carefully bathed it, dressed it in shrouds, and kept it company until burial, so the soul would be comforted in its return to the Almighty, *reboyne-sheloylam.* Burial was always within twenty-four hours of death, and woe unto you if you died on a Friday, because keeping the *shabes* was a holier requirement. A hurried burial before sundown, or another day of *shmire* until the funeral. Coffins, if used, were simple wooden boxes, no metal fastenings, always kept closed. When lowered into the ground, the first shovels of earth were dropped by the closest relatives. After reciting *Kaddish,* the bereaved went home, lit the memorial candle that would burn throughout the *shiva,* seven days of tears and letting go. Thirty days of mourning, a moon's full cycle, before coming back to resume the everyday. After a whole year of days that began with *glorified and sanctified is the Holy Name . . . ,* the dead were finally put to rest, and remembered each year with *yortsayt,* the anniversary of the death.

In that loose-leaf binder in the cemetery shed, filled with mimeographed and handwritten pages, was this fragment, from a local newspaper, circa 1960:

> " . . . *little grave houses to preserve loved ones*
> *from the ravages of wild animals and spirits* . . . "

How difficult it must have been to bury the dead in winter, to dig the frozen earth. The digging couldn't have gone down very deep. Was this the explanation for the grave houses? But what about the idea of "spirits"? It didn't ring Yiddish in my ears.

For Jews, the key word is soul, not spirit. It's not that we have souls, we are souls, content in our closeness to *reboyne-sheloylam*. We cry when The Almighty, Master of the Universe, sends us for our time on earth.

Then, the great forgetting.

Attached to earthly life, a soul can be frightened to leave its body. Thus the mitzvah of *shmire,* fulfilled by the *Khevra Kadisha,* of keeping the soul company, easing the journey home to *reboyne-sheloylam.*

And the murals recently painted on the façade of Lipton's old hotel? I'd seen them on the way to the cemetery. The central panel showed a Jew in a black hat, wrapped in a blanket – or was it a *tallis?* – with a teepee in the background. Was there indeed a relationship between the Jewish settlers and the native people, already treatied onto reserves not far away?

Such silence about the Cree and Métis people. Hardly mentioned in the Jewish memoirs I read, or in the recollections of the descendents of the settlers that I sought out to interview. Why these grave houses? I asked. To protect the bodies from wild beasts, I was told.

Feeling my way back to the past, fingers groping for roots,
roots become fingers.

In *The Dominion of the Dead,* Robert Pogue Harrison asks:
Why did the living house the dead before they housed themselves?

*To inhabit the world humanly, one must be a creature of legacy. We, the
living, are but the ligature between the dead
and the unborn.*

Our deepest human impulse – perpetuation of our existence
beyond death – expressed through a house of memory,
a house of bones.

To die childless, the worst Jewish tragedy.

Who will say Kaddish?

Kaddish, our ligature.

My murdered family, some buried alive, others in unknown mass graves, forbidden to leave a trace. Robbed of their lives, robbed of their deaths. And me, robbed of both. With no place to go to remember them, no place to say, here they lived and died, and here am I, come from them. I may never have visited those graves, but I need to know that they existed. Their graves the proof of their existence. All my life, this rootlessness. I had come from the Shoah's fire, come from vapor, but not from earth.

In the year I said Kaddish for my father, my mother asked me to design his tombstone. It would be simple, modest in decoration, but would record these essential facts: *Eliyahu*, his Hebrew name; the names of his parents, *Yisroel*, the Cohen, and Esther Leah Lewin; the places and dates that he entered and left this world; and the central mark of his life, the barbed lines of the *Mogen David*, inscribed where his heart would be. And carved in the stone above, in remembrance of his priestly caste, two hands, forming a triangle, fingers splayed in benediction. My father, a son of the sons of Aaron, of the people Israel, buried in Miami, the 22nd of the month of *Shevat*, in the year 5757.

Besoylem, Yiddish, cemetery

From Hebrew, *bayit,* a house; *olam,* the world, universe, eternity

Besoylem, House of Eternity, House of the World to Come *(olam haba)*

(Why did the living house their dead before they housed themselves?)

The dead need a house for the work they must do.

The work of the dead?

Intercede on behalf of the living, *olam hazeh.*

Bridge.

How could the stunned Jewish arrivals to the Qu'Appelle Valley have survived, if not by learning from the native people?

How did the Cree and Métis bury their dead?

The Plains Cree, written in the thirties by David Mandelbaum, offered this:

> *"The Calling River People, now on the Crooked Lake reserves, erect small gable-roofed board houses over the graves . . ."*

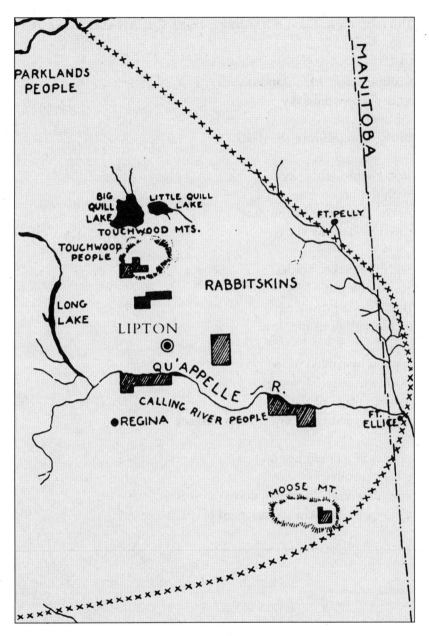

DETAIL OF MANDELBAUM'S MAP SHOWING RANGE OF PLAINS CREE
AS OF 1860–1870. SHADED AREAS ARE RESERVES OF PLAINS CREE AS OF 1936.

Photograph, Cree Cemetery, Fort Qu'Appelle, May 1885

Calling River Man stands guard
under a brooding sky
a barren valley
in the dominion of the dead

under a brooding sky
within a picket border
in the dominion of the dead
tiny wooden dwellings

within a picket border
topped by gabled roofs
tiny wooden dwellings
a cold village of the dead

topped by gabled roofs
plain and painted houses
a cold village of the dead
complete with windows, doors, crosses

plain and painted houses
a barren valley
complete with windows, doors, crosses
Calling River Man stands guard

CREE CEMETERY, FORT QU'APPELLE, MAY 1885.

IMMIGRANT SONG
Lipton Cemetery

As if I heard a drum
struck by an invisible hand,
as if after thirty years in Canada
the grass sang me a welcome song.

As if those Jewish bones called me
meydele, said they'd waited for me so long,
as if they laid their hands on my eyes
to unblind me, and pulled me close to listen
as they whispered fragments of their stories,
slices of their dreams, as if

their little village of spirit houses
was tired of silence,
as if their gables pointed to the Calling River People,
as if my heart unlocked the door of its spirit house
and set off to find the letters
painted on tin, chiselled in stone,
bleached by sun,
blown by snowfall,
to gather them home.

The Pale

My Mother Spits on Tzar Nikolai

I hear my mother say *Tzar Nikolai,* the hiss of *tz* like a lit fuse,
then the *k* and *ai* swiftly exploding.

She had plenty of reason to detest the first Tzar Nikolai, and
the second, and the Alexanders in between. All despised the
Jews, wanted to be rid of them. Catherine the Great was the
first to solve it – the Pale of Settlement. They swept the Jews,
homegrown and acquired, into the swath of land stretching
from the Baltic to the Black Sea. Expelled from cities, relegated
to small towns, huddled in miserable *stetlekh,* forbidden from
owning or leasing land, told what they could and couldn't do,
from sunrise to sunrise.

Tzar Nikolai took the prize – over 600 laws against the Jews,
the worst of all – conscription, 1825, the year of his crown. All
Jewish boys from age eight or nine were game to be plucked,
handed to the Russian army, to serve for twenty-five. Quotas
had to be filled, the Jews had to fill them. Punishments were
severe. Jewish kidnappers – *khappers* – snatched little boys,
pouncing like cougars, dragging off their prey. The idea:
brutalize the Jews within their communities, continue by
decimating their young. Deracinate them, torture them into
renouncing their religion, enslave them twenty-five years,
and *ot azoy* is the Jewish soul destroyed.

My mother heard it all from her *heylikn zeydn.* He'd been
khapped from his home around 1860, a boy of eight or nine,
into the Russian army for twenty-five. His birthplace, birthdate,
names of his parents, a mystery still. The greater mystery –
how blood and fire forged his *Yiddishe neshume.*

TZAR NIKOLAI

snatched my great-grandfather Mordechai,
a boy of eight years, shackled him
for twenty-five.
Tzar Nikolai stuffed his boots with straw, marched him
'til the snow turned red, raised his whip
to remove all trace of home,
the feel of his spoon, the taste
of borscht, the sound of his
father calling him
for *ma'ariv* prayers.

After one thousand nights
of secret *shema yisroel,*
(adonai elokainu adonai ekhad)
shivering on the barn's hard floor,
the outline of his mother's face,
behind his eyes,

                erased.

After five thousand
she became song,
a nign, a zmire,
Shekhina
the *shabes* queen.

After 1881, the Year of the Tzar's Assassination

Pogrom: 1882, Yiddish
From Russian *pogromu,* "devastation, destruction,"
from *po* – "by, through" and *gromu* – "thunder, roar"

A Yiddish word, *pogrom,* sprung from the Russian, from thunder,
from roar. The oldest story, hatred and destruction. To run for
your life your only escape.

Five million Jews in the Pale of Settlement, *tsezeyt un tseshpreyt.*
More than two hundred communities suffered destruction, while
world organizations scrambled to aid. Outrage was heard from
cities across Europe. The US opened its doors.

In thirty-three years, one in three Jews
of eastern Europe left their homeland,
crossed an ocean, washed ashore.

Canada's west cried out for people,
      investment was needed for the CPR.
Invite a few refugees to settle?
Would Rothschild repay kindness with funding for the rail?

Alexander Galt, Canada's High Commissioner to London,
to John A. Macdonald, Prime Minister:

> *I am discussing with the Jews . . .*
> *an exodus from Russia to Canada . . .*
> *How would you like an influx of Ole Clo?*

John A. Macdonald to Alexander Galt:

> *A sprinkling of Jews in the North West*
> *would do much good. They would at once*
> *go in for peddling and politics . . .*

Alexander Galt to John A. Macdonald:

> *I have made contact with Lord Rothschild . . .*

BARON AND BARONESS DE HIRSCH

My son I have lost, but not my heir; humanity is my heir
— BARON MAURICE DE HIRSCH, 1887

Maurice and Clara, a golden couple of the gilded age,
their evenings, tuxedos and damask gowns

waltzing ballrooms of Brussels, Paris,
glittering theatres of crystal chandeliers.

His days, in his office, with the Turkish sultan,
pressing the seal for the railway to Constantinople,

hers, funding almshouses, soup kitchens,
clothing for children, loans for the poor.

She can't live her life of splendour
without sharing her wealth, her example

to her husband: give more, give even more.
The cries of their people trapped in the

Pale, ring louder, the streets of Moscow,
Kiev shriek blood and thunder.

They cry in private; no potion
can quell the pain

of burying your one and only child.
Clara now dresses in mourning clothes,

Maurice, at her bidding, devotes his millions
to the rescue of his people:

creates schools, teaches farming,
sends them to lands

of freedom.
Gives them tools.

A Few Restrictions Regarding the Jews
of Romania, 1885–1900

a restriction forbidding Jews to be peddlers
a restriction forbidding Jews to be shopkeepers
a restriction forbidding Jews to sell tobacco
a restriction forbidding Jews to sell cakes or sugar
a restriction forbidding Jews from being innkeepers
a restriction forbidding Jews to sell alcohol
a restriction forbidding Jews from elementary school
a restriction forbidding Jews from upper school,
  agricultural school, trade school
a restriction forbidding Jews to open their own schools
a restriction forbidding Jews from being military officers
a restriction forbidding Jews from being journalists
a restriction forbidding Jews from being clerks
a restriction forbidding Jews from being craftsmen
a restriction forbidding Jews from being pharmacists,
a restriction forbidding Jews to practice medicine
a restriction forbidding Jews to work in mental hospitals
a restriction forbidding Jews to be patients in hospitals
a restriction forbidding Jews from owning land
a restriction forbidding Jews from cultivating land
a restriction forbidding Jews from working for a farmer
a restriction forbidding Jews from being citizens

To escape Romania, put one foot
in front of the other,
only walk in groups,
carry a song, give a performance.
On a broadside write:
> "*With heavy hearts we leave the land of our fathers
> to wander in foreign places.
> We have drunk the last bitter drops from the cup
> of suffering.*"

Go from *shtetl* to *shtetl*,
hope for a bowl of soup,
a few *bani,* a *shtikl broyt.*
If possible, bring another pair of shoes,
a book, a photograph for *gedenken,*
walk all day, make the fields your bed,
dream some nights you'll be offered a bath,
expect the passing of two full moons.
Aim for the Austro-Hungarian border,
south through the Carpathians,
or north through Bukovina,
board a train for Hamburg or Rotterdam,
believe that Baron de Hirsch will provide
for this ticket, and the next,
for steerage to London,
train to Liverpool, then ship,
for the ocean crossing,
the final leg,
to Canada,
tsezeyt un tseshpreyt
into the wilderness.

The Forest Prays

Early one morning, he ran into the deepest woods
My neighbor learned of his parent's death in Romania
He wished to say *Kaddish* but there was no *minyan*
Curious, I followed at a distance

My neighbor learned of his parent's death in Romania
He paused and grasped a tree with extreme devotion
Curious, I followed at a distance
Loudly he chanted *yisgadal v'yiskadash shemay raba*

He paused and grasped a tree with extreme devotion
Snowy leaves, made light by the frost, flew in the air like feathers
Loudly he chanted *yisgadal v'yiskadash shemay raba*
It seemed as if souls long departed were present

Snowy leaves, made light by the frost, flew in the air like feathers
I answered together with the whole forest
It seemed as if souls long departed were present
I could swear the trees trembled, the whole forest prayed

I answered together with the whole forest
He wished to say *Kaddish* but there was no *minyan*
I could swear the trees trembled, the whole forest prayed
Early one morning he ran into the deepest woods

Frequently Asked Questions

JEWISH SETTLERS' F.A.Q.S

In Yiddish, a pamphlet

vikhtike fragen, rikhtige entfers

important questions, correct answers,

for those who are thinking of

basetzn zikh oyfn land een Kanade

to set themselves,

to sit,

to plant.

וואו געפינט זיך דאס לאנד וועלכעס די קאנאדישע רעגירונג גיט פריי?

Where is the land located which the Canadian Government
is granting free?

> West of Lake Superior, north of Minnesota, North Dakota,
> east of the Rocky Mountains, in the provinces of Manitoba,
> Saskatchewan and Alberta.

וואס פיר איין לאנד איז דאס?

What kind of land is this?

> The land is very good, mostly open prairie with some
> dense wooded areas. Generally the soil is black and from
> one to three feet deep.

A Pioneer Girl's Diary: July 1887

The first to show were crocus,
mauve anemones in fur coats
then clusters of purple violets,
orange cowslips, yellow pea blossoms
on a long white stem,
tufts of purple not unlike thistle,
a low vine of coral hollyhock.

Wild tomatoes, taste of copper penny
in your mouth, ground plums, magenta,
shooting star.
Blue gentians,
blue stars on the grass,
dainty bluebells,
a haze of blue all about.

Roses, white and blue asters
in three different kinds,
wild sage with purplish bergamot,
white yarrow, wormwood,
fireweed.

אויב דאס לאנד איז גוט ווארום גיט עס די רעגירונג אוועק פריי?

If the land is good, why is the government granting it free?

Canada is 3,729,665 square miles and the population is still very small. The government understands that the country can become rich and strong through development of its agriculture.

וי אזוי איז דאס לאנד צעטיילט?

How is the Land Divided?

All of the agricultural land in the three provinces of
Saskatchewan, Alberta and Manitoba are divided into
squares six miles long by six miles wide and each square
is called a township. Each township is divided into thirty-
six smaller squares which are called sections. Each section
of one mile holds six hundred and forty acres. The sections
are numbered from one to thirty-six. Each section is
divided into four equal parts which are called quarter
sections. Each quarter section is one half mile in size and
holds one hundred and sixty acres. That is the number
of acres which the Government is granting free. When we
refer to homestead or farm we mean one hundred and sixty
acres of land. Each section is one square and has four sides,
east, west, north and south. When we refer to a quarter
section you must also state the direction of it – northeast,
northwest, southeast, or southwest. To make this clearer,
we have drawn a plan of a township and a plan for a
section.

Plan of Township 22

range 13 west of second meridian

rolling country timbered with fine bluffs of poplar,
    numerous hay marshes

    explanation of colours:

    woods, green;
    scrub or prairie and woods, dotted green;
    water, blue;
    marshes, yellow with small strokes of black;
    hills or slopes, etching or grey shade;
    brule (burnt woods), brown;
    settler's improvements, pink.

DEPARTMENT OF THE INTERIOR

Topographical Surveys Branch
Ottawa, 17th October, 1892

approved and confirmed

PLAN OF TOWNSHIP 22 RANGE 13 WEST OF SECOND MERIDIAN

SECOND EDITION (CORRECTED)

Scale: 40 Chains to an inch.

EXPLANATION OF COLOURS: Woods, green; scrub or prairie woods, dotted green; water, blue; marshes, yellow with small strokes of black; hills or slopes, etching or grey shade; brule (burnt woods), brown; settler's improvements, pink.

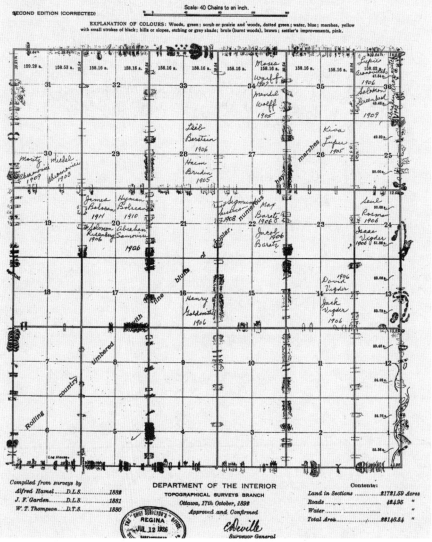

Compiled from surveys by
Alfred Hamel......D.L.S...............1882
J. F. Garden......D.L.S...............1881
W. T. Thompson......D.T.S...............1880

DEPARTMENT OF THE INTERIOR
TOPOGRAPHICAL SURVEYS BRANCH
Ottawa, 17th October, 1892
Approved and Confirmed

E. Deville
Surveyor General

Contents:
Land in Sections ....21721.59 Acres
Roads .... 424.95 "
Water .... "
Total Area................22146.54 "

ווי לאַנג דויערט דער ווינטער?

How long is the winter season?

The snow starts around November and disappears around
the beginning of April. Alberta is warmer than Manitoba
and Saskatchewan.

LIARS

Ligners, ligners	liars, liars	ליגנערס, ליגנערס
Shney in der sukkele,	snow in the sukka	שניי אין דער סוכלה
Shney bis shvuos	snow til Shavuot	שניי ביז שבועות
A finstere kholem	a nightmare	א פינצטערער חלום

איז פאראן גענוג רעגען?

Is there enough rain?

> Usually there is enough rain except some years
> in the eastern areas where there is less rainfall.

וואספארא צייט הויבט מען אן צו זעען?

When can one start to sow seed?

> Usually at the beginning of April,
>> but sometimes not till late in May.

וואס פאר א תבואה וואקסט אין קאנאדא?

What kind of crops grow in Canada?

> Wheat, oats, barley, flax, rye and others.

A thing of beauty cut from ash

the straightest branch, a long arm

sturdy hand of steel joined to wood

fingers curved from an open palm

a thing of beauty I tell you

the heft and fit so right

my back tipped forward, arms

swoop and arc, golden straw

caught in the tines,   toss, release

a thing of beauty

over and over

stooks rise in the baking sun

ווי לאַנג דויערט עס ביז ווייץ ווערט פאַרטיג?

How long does it take for wheat to grow?

From 100–125 days.

קען מען דאָס ערשטע יאָהר האָבען אַן אוראָזשאַי,ערנטע?

Can one have a crop harvest the first year?

You can but it is not advisable because the land is
very wild and has to be strongly cultivated the first year.

RED HARVEST

Mostly we feared

the red cloud

rising

when we bound

our wheat

          into sheaves

rust bit the stems

rotten

made hunger

our winter

Manager Baker Explains the Causes of Discontent Among Settlers — the Advances Made

Reports of trouble amongst the settlers in the Baron Hirsch Colony have been rife.

There have been some ugly rumors as to discontent amongst the settlers. Is there any truth in these reports?

Well, yes, there have been symptoms of discontent, and I might explain to you the cause.

They wanted pay for the time they had worked before being supplied with their oxen, horses, etc.

They had come out ignorant of farming, and to help them three instructors were hired to teach them how to plough, etc., at a cost of $400.

During the time from May till the 1st of July they pretended to work and with a large number of teams succeeded in breaking forty acres, about as much as one good man and a good team would do in the time.

The wives and families of the first settlers were kept in Montreal for twenty-four weeks, and nothing was charged them for clothing or food in all that time.

Their grounds of discontent were these: (1) They wanted to be provided for one year more. (2) Wanted farm implements, etc., in addition to what they had already received. (3) Wanted compensation for time lost by not being able to commence work immediately on their arrival. This was practically impossible.

What charges were made them for provisions? Did they get them at cost? Yes, at wholesale cost:

Tea at 25 cents, sugar 20 pounds for $1, and other things in proportion.

In large families of say six children and parents, a sack of flour per week was supplied, and a pound of rice and pound of sugar per head, in fact, amply sufficient for their needs, as their present condition will prove.

It would appear that the only thing wrong with the people is that they are too well treated, and that they should be taught that they will need to at least make some efforts to help themselves. What are the prospects for a crop this year?

We have suffered from drought this season, replied Mr. Baker, and except in the northern part of the colony there will be very little.

from a newspaper account

וואָס פֿאַר אַ גאַרטעגנוואַרג וואַקסען דאָרט?

What kind of garden plants grow there?

Potatoes, rape, carrots, beets, onions,
cabbage, radish, peas and so on.

kartofel, tzibele,	potato, onion	קאַרטאָפֿל, זיבעלה
ugerke, kroyt,	pickle, cabbage	אוגערקה, קרויט
zovere kroyt,	sauerkraut	זוויערע קרויט
a bissel shmaltz,	a little chicken fat	אַ ביסל שמאַלץ
gepregelte tzibele,	fried onions	גפֿרעגלטע ציבעלה
a sthikl broyt,	a piece of bread	אַ שטיקל ברויט
royte borikes	red beets	רויטע בוריקעס
kartofel mit lupeh,	potatoes in their skins	קאַרטאָפֿל מיט לופֿע
a sheyne borscht,	a beautiful borscht	אַ שיינע באָרשט
a likhtik yohr	a bright year	אַ ליכטיק יאָר

וואקסען אויך פרוכטען?

Can you grow fruit?

    Only small wild fruits.

I loved it. The grain, the cattle, the chickens, the sky, the berries in the field, strawberries, raspberries, gooseberries, saskatoons, chokeberries.

– MAGGIE WASSERMAN BROWNSTONE,
UNPUBLISHED DIARY

LIL SCHACTER AND CLAIRE SHAFFER, TWO SISTERS
IN THEIR NINETIES, REMINISCE:

*In 1901 our parents left Romania. We don't know why they chose
Lipton, but that's where they came. Dug a hole to bury their
belongings the first winter. Where else could they put their things?*

*Then we had two houses made of mud, with wooden floors. One for
sleeping, the other, where we ate. Our Bubbe baked challeh and pletzl
for breakfast. Even the children drank coffee, our national drink.
Every week, before shabes, we'd have our baths. All clean, wrapped
in a towel, carried between our mud houses. After all this time,
this memory is so clear.*

*We didn't stay too long on the homestead. We moved to Lipton.
Father opened a store.*

INTERVIEWED IN VICTORIA, 2003.

קאָנגרייגיישען תפארת ישראל דליפטאן קאָלאני

מרדכי ברונשטיין	1	
יכתיאל יאמפאלסקי	2	
צבי יאמפאלסקי	3	
יונה יאמפאלסקי	4	
ישיהו נומארק	5	
מאיר פעקיט	6	
יצחק פישערמאן	7	
חיים מאיאוויטש	8	
אייזיק פינקלער	9	
יוסף פאקשאנער	10	
קלאצמאן	11	
יעקב זיסקרויט	12	
אריה דוב סאנגורסקי	13	
ישראל וויינער	14	

A PAGE FROM THE LEDGER OF CONGREGATION TIFERES YISROEL, LIPTON.

COLONISTS OF CONGREGATION *Tiferes Yisroel de Lipton*

Mordechai Bronstein

Yichtiel Yampolski

Tzvi Yampolski

Yonah Yampolski

Yishaiya Neumark

Meier Pechet

Yitzhak Fisherman

Chaim Mayavitz

Itzik Sinclair

Yoseph Fakshaner

Klatzman

Yakov Ziskraut

Aryeh Dov Pangorski

Yisroel Weiner

a page from the ledger

וואס זענען די באדינגונגען פאר דעם יידישן ערד ארבעטער?

What is it like for the Jewish farmer?

> Jewish farmers live mostly in colonies, that is groups
> and not in towns, because according to the law every
> farmer who gets free land from the government must
> live on the land. They support teachers, ritual slaughterers
> and in older colonies they also have synagogues and
> charity loan societies. They get together from time to
> time whenever possible for an evening of entertainment
> and interesting discussion on agriculture and how to
> improve their situations.

from Wm. J. Grutchfield.

Dear Sir.

I have been left in charge of the Hirsch Jewish Colony Supply Store for the past three months and the supplies have run out as there was not much left in store when W. H. Baker left me in charge and as I have written repeatedly to Montreal and can get no satisfaction what to give the colonists I thought it advisable to let you know the state of affairs. I have every reason to believe that a great many of the people are in want of food & fuel and I think if there is not something done at once on behalf of these people there will be some sickness and probably death amongst them. I do not know what the committee intend doing in the matter, but I cannot hold myself responsible for anything that may happen through want or exposure as I have no money or authority to buy food for these people. If you would kindly inform me how to act in this matter I would be very thankful and will also be very much obliged if you will favor me with reply. I am yours respectfully. Wm Grutchfield

וואָס דאַרף אַ מעגטש טאָן אויב ער האָט ניט קיין דערפאַרונג אין
ערד אַרבעט?

What does a man do if he has no experience in farming?

> We advise anyone who has decided to become a farmer
> in Canada and does not have the necessary experience,
> to hire out for one year to an experienced farmer to
> gain the knowledge for farming.

ADVICE FROM A GRANDFATHER, A RABBI, TO HIS GRANDSON, AGE 14, LEAVING RUSSIA ON HIS OWN, FOR CANADA, 1909:

My boy, you will be living amongst strangers and you must remember that when a stranger offers you the privilege of eating at his table, you must respect his customs and eat his food. If you are invited to eat with a gentile, it is not considered a sin to remove your hat. You may take your hat off out of respect of your host. You may find yourself at a table with food that is forbidden to us. You can avoid those foods if you know about them but if you don't, do not insult your host by refusing them. It is more important to respect other people's customs and their ways of life than to persist in your own ways and customs. People abuse the privileges of their religious training or customs and show disrespect for others by inflicting them on unwilling neighbours, as well as throwing doubt on one's own intelligence.

From *Mendel's Children,*
a memoir by Cherie Smith

Sukkele

HIS PROMISE

Like Adam and Chava,
we'd make our own *gan eydn,*
live in a sturdy cabin, filled with
moonlight. God's light at last
come out from hiding.

I held my breath
across the ocean,
would have broken
the ice with my own hands
to finally enter Halifax harbour

then lost count of days riding
on wooden benches, every bone
raw from rocking, as iron wheels
roared across a grassy sea

and I thought,
how vast this earth, how far
a smallness, me, can go,
and looking up this boundless sky,
imagined going this same distance, up,
beyond the blue, imagined going past the stars
I couldn't name, imagined no end at all,
but was confused by this brief consolation,

for each mile confirmed my muffled fear

what I've left behind I'll never hold again.

How strange to find him
dressed in fur and skins,
face dark from dirt and beard
not scrubbed nor shaved.
When he smiled I recognized
we were strangers now.

He brought me to a house of
mudded blocks cut straight from earth.
My thin suit no shield
against the wind,
I lay down on our bed of straw
and wept
as moonlight flooded in.

When the Grass First Felt the Plough

I.

Late afternoon,
chalcedony and flint sent flying by the harrow

feet shod in old country leather, broken
by thousands of miles of heel strike,
swollen flesh.

To them, the prairie,
a vast fallow sea and
unknown song,
an open palm.

II.

Evening,
we pull quartz from our pockets,
pale blue, glowing like moonstone, a waxy light

learn words to stand for distance,

                              (prairie)

for heart squeeze,

                              (mother's wave goodbye)

for earth house

sod,

while through the gape called

window

coyote shadow flickers past,   unnamed.

HUSBANDRY

In any case, we knew *gornisht*.
Not the cost of a pound of seed.
Nor with what to buy it.
Nor how to break the ground to offer it.
We opened our mouths
and sounds flew out like black wings
beating fast into sky.
Whoosh. Whoosh.
A mass of dark wings
a cold silver sky.

We dug out the earth
and lay down in it.
Sha shtil.
His hand to my mouth.
Barely more than a *kind*.
A *vaybele.*
I knew nothing.
His hand where I couldn't even
touch myself. My heart
a horse running over frozen ground.
His flesh burning into me.
With whom could I speak of these things?

Of how a man plants his seed,
and the moon grows full, then dark,
then full again.

LAUNDRY DAY

Most appalling
the piles of dirty overalls,
underwear, linens, shirts and socks,
the pails of boiling water
carried heavy from stove
to stuffed iron tubs
and despite our care,
countless blisters
from our spills.

Most astonishing
the smell of clean,
rising from the bushes and rocks,
(our corsets and bloomers tucked
into pillow slips, out of sight)
the pleasure we'd sneak
lying in summer grass,
faces flushed with sun,
before mosquitoes drove us
back to our chores.

Folk Remedies*

To speed childbirth: drink a tea of partridge berry leaves
    for several weeks

To promote rapid delivery: swallow an infusion of blue
    cohosh root for several weeks

To speed delivery of placenta: offer a tea made
    from boiled licorice roots

To stop postpartum hemorrhage: give chokecherry juice

To ease the pain of childbirth: sip wild black cherry

For infant colic: spoonfuls of catnip leaf tea

Abortificant: try rue

* *lost source*

My Mother's *Sukkele* Song

A sukkele a kleyne	A very small sukka
fun breytlekh gemeyne	from cheap planks,
hob ikh mir mit tzores gemakht	I struggled to make
Fardekt dem dakh	I covered the roof
mit a bisele skhakh	with a few branches,
zits ikh mir een sukkele bey nakht	and sit in my sukka each night
Der vint, der kalter	A cold wind
er blost durkh di shpaltn	blows through the cracks
oysleshn mayne likhtelekh er vil	and wants to blow out my lights
Es iz mir a khidesh	For me it's quite amazing
vi ikh shtey un makh Kiddush	that I can make Kiddush,
un de likhtelekh brenen ruyig un shtil	and the lights continue to glow
Dos ershte gerikht,	With a pained look on her face,
mit a troyerik gezikht	the first course
trogt mir mayn vaybele arayn	is brought in by my dear wife
Zi shtelt zikh avek,	She stands nearby,
un zogt mir mit shrek	and says with great fear
"der vint varft dayn sukke bald ayn"	"the wind is blowing the sukka down!"
Zay nisht keyn nar	Don't be a fool,
un hob nisht keyn tzar	don't be sad,
zol dir di sukke nisht ton bang	don't be upset about the sukka
Vintn zey kumen	Winds come,
zey blozn zey brumen	they blow and roar
dokh shtayt shoyn mayn sukkele	but my sukka keeps standing
ganz lang	
Es is shoyn gor	It's already been
bald tsvey toyznt yor	two thousand years,
un di sukkele zi shteyt nokh ganz lang	and the sukka is still standing

Harvest Festival Song

Our *sukkele* song
from this promised land

a different song
for our soddy "booths"

their grassy crowns unkempt
after summer's long radiance.

At harvest time we barber
our roofs' long tresses

rejoice and remember
our *sukkeles* built

as God commanded,
with roofs of living branches

protected
by the light of stars.

We share bread from our fields,
drink chokecherry wine

glistening rubies plucked
by the riverbanks

sing: *hazorim bedimah, berinah yiktzoru*
        those who sow in tears, will reap with joy

count the years in the thousands
forbidden to plough and to harvest

but always we remembered,
forty years in the desert

as God required –
our slave-husks baked brittle

before cracking open
                              shed

Bridges

STEPPING BACK THROUGH THE GATE

In 2005, one hundred years after the North-West Territories traded its name for Saskatchewan and became a province of Canada, and two years after I'd first stepped foot in the Lipton Hebrew Cemetery, I journeyed back to visit the sites of the Jewish colonies. I'd spent time in the archives, read some history, many memoirs, and listened to voices of some who'd been born there. I'd also spent much time talking with my mother, whose startling memory allowed her to recreate her childhood in Poland in great detail. I imagined myself making the journey the colonists made. Imagined what I'd find.

I travelled with Hilary, a transplanted Zimbabwean, who, intrigued by my request, volunteered to be my travel companion. We shared a respect for cemeteries, and awe for the natural world. But she could spot a Swainson's hawk before a dark speck even registered in my eye, and knew the names of almost everything that grew around us. We set off on a two thousand kilometre drive, circling from Regina to Lipton, north to Edenbridge on the Carrot River, then south to Wapella, Rocanville, and west to Hirsch, and Sonnenfeld. Four days packed with wonder.

After we parted, I journeyed on to St. Peter's monastery in Muenster, for my first sojourn at the writer's colony. Where I began to write it down.

BRIDGES

The entire world is a narrow bridge
— REB NACHMAN OF BRATZSLAV

Bernadette, riding in her beat-up Pontiac, from Regina to
St. Peter's, windows rolled down and hair streaming
as we told our stories,

hers beginning on the family farm, in Earl Grey,
a mere hawk's swoop from Lipton,
but she knew nothing of its Jewish past, was taken aback.
Her family's farmed there for three generations.

We came from Bukovina, she said, but I'm not sure where
that is, somewhere near Austria, I've been told, or maybe
even Russia.

It rang a bell, cracked, but echoing, faintly, of Romania.

We came from that part of the world where borders keep
on changing. My parents born in Poland, but these days it's
Belarus and Ukraine. I was born in Germany after the war.
Grew up in Boston.

My family's German Lutheran, Bernadette says.

The question I always ask myself, the one I can't understand

How could my people

Bernadette, here's a story from my mother.

A German officer was billeted in her Warsaw apartment the first week of the war. He was a fine man, kind and courteous. They shared their chaste longings, his for his wife and child, hers for her husband who'd left to visit home in that last week of August.

Shortly after, the German officer was posted elsewhere.

One night, after curfew, my mother was trapped on the wrong side of the bridge she had to cross to get home. Shaking in fear for her life, she heard the officer's voice call out:

> Frau Milman, *bitte,* I will take you across.

Amber Raspberries

I met Father Martin on my second day at St. Peter's, a
Benedictine colony that was lured from its home in Minnesota
in 1903. Land was free for religious colonies too. I had no
knowledge of this history when I arrived; I knew nothing about
St. Peter's, other than as a place that housed a writer's colony for
a few weeks every summer. Not the college it ran, nor the dairy
and poultry it raised, the acres of organic wheat it grew, along
with tons of potatoes and bushels of corn. Its kitchen gardens,
bordered by sunflowers and sweet peas, supplied fresh summer
bounties, fruit of the monks' hard labour, all done between prayers.
This monastic life attracts seekers still, as it has for many centuries.

I met him as he zoomed out of the graveyard on his golf cart.
I needed a break from translation and writing, and wanted to
discover where I'd landed. "Hop on," he waved to me. "Let's go
pick amber raspberries. I'll show you where to find the best
raspberries of all." We'd had amber raspberries for dinner the
previous evening, and never had I tasted raspberries so sweet and
seed-free. I didn't expect to be led to the source of this treasure.

Doing 50 on the golf cart, as we bumped and dipped over
tractor tracks, I squashed my misgivings and hung on. Soon
enough, we arrived at the patch, and dismounted. He asked me
to stand back for a moment, while he grabbed his walking sticks
and swung them like golf clubs, whacking shoulder-high thistles
in our path. "Now we can have a closer reach."

We started picking, while exchanging the basics: name, family,
home, mission, and so moved down the row, from English to a
bit of German, his childhood tongue, and me responding in a
rusty Yiddish, my almost extinguished *mameloshn*. But we had no
trouble understanding each other in the three languages we
pushed around with our tongues, already happily stained by

berries. "So you're writing a book about the Jewish farmers of Saskatchewan." "Here, four berries, under this leaf," he pointed.

He was nearly ninety, his birthday coming up in October. Seventy-five years at the abbey. His brother Gregory, three months past his hundredth birthday, was buried in the cemetery just three weeks before. The third of four Brodners of St. Peter's. Only Martin now left. On the way back ("if you lean forward in your seat, you won't fall off," he assured me) we tucked into the cemetery to visit John, George and Gregory, whose freshly dug grave needed a cross, which he drew with his cane, in the dry brown dirt.

Their family came from Bukovina, around 1905. He was born on their homestead, in Dysart, one of the youngest of fifteen children. He still remembered the Jewish shopkeepers in Dysart: Yampoulski/Sangourski/Weiner/Geebes. My ears tingled – I'd just translated these names from the Yiddish pages of the Lipton Colony Ledger. This history suddenly so close and real. "They knew we had a big family, so they took good care of us. We were poor." He was excited now, my mission releasing childhood memories that blew up all around us, like spikelets of speargrass set in flight by his whacking sticks. "I have a book about the Jews of Lipton, and you must have it."

That afternoon, sitting in the pews at the organ concert, I leafed through *The Light of Israel,* their book of psalms, and read the English versions of my Hebrew childhood prayers. It surprised me to see these Jewish prayers, with no acknowledgement of origins. The hated authors of the exalted word. Organ music has never agreed with me, but I had decided to go to the concert, to test out the experience. I found myself sitting opposite Father Martin. With eyes closed, I floated up with the music, my thoughts mingled with tears in the crevices of mind that bordered language. Feelings foreshadowing words.

Later, at dinnertime, we were surprised with an invitation to dine with the monks. After a meal of chicken, mashed potatoes and cabbage slaw, and with permission, I went to Father Martin's table. He was eager to receive me.

"I checked with my niece in Dysart, and she confirmed that the book was in the box of belongings I packed up after Brother Gregory's death. What will I do with this book, I asked myself, and so I sent it on. But I'll do my best to get it back for you before you leave. I promise."

When I mentioned the Psalms of Israel, he told me they are his life. Morning, noon and vespers the monks sing them, completing them all in a two-week cycle, when they start again. "If you come to Vespers, you can hear them."

"My brother Gregory had a beautiful book of Psalms, which I have in my possession, and the book must now belong to you."

His brother. Just died. His psalms. As Father Martin's surprisingly powerful hand gripped my arm, I felt a passage of sheer love, a *coup de foudre* of soul contact, made even more potent as I heard my mother's words lilting in the air around us. I had phoned her on Friday, for our weekly conversation, and as we wished each other a *gut shabes,* I told her I'd be at the abbey. "It would be very familiar to me, from my childhood in Pohorolowka," she said. "I know all their songs."

Pohorolowka, how I love the sound of that mythical village, where the family flour mill stood, where the three Jewish families were loved and belonged, where life was good.

I needed to learn more about Bukovina, Father Martin's family home, and Bernadette's too. As if there was a reason it kept coming up on this pilgrimage. I could hardly picture Bukovina on a map, its location as vague to me as countless other regions of Europe where boundaries were ripped up and redrawn in blood. The Reader's Digest World Atlas listed it as a historical entity, with no direction to any map. The Britannica sent me to the History of the Balkans, which I thought was a wild goose chase, but sure enough, there was Bukovina, a little shape-shifting pouch of land, bulging north from Romania's belly, in the shadow of the Carpathian mountains. Here so many ancient rivals – Ukranians, Poles, Germans, Slovaks, Bessarabians, Moldovans, Bulgarians and Turks – elbowed and tugged for their portion, right into this most vicious of centuries. And living amongst them, for more than seven centuries, as usual in Central and Eastern Europe, were Jews. Then. Pohorolowka was not very far away.

Next morning, I printed out a photograph that I took of Father Martin at the berry patch, and brought it to him, along with a copy of my first book of poems. He in turn presented me with a picture of Anne Frank, tucked inside Brother Gregory's book of Psalms, which he'd highlighted with his favourite passages. Each of us had inscribed, on the inside cover, "in remembrance of amber raspberries."

POSTCARD TO ANNE FRANK ON JUNE 12TH, OUR BIRTHDAY

Why me in this life?
Why not you?

Twenty years
a gray shiver of time
between our comings.

Today, in a poem I found:
"In the dark, my soul said
I am your soul."

Do souls grow old?
Has yours
come into my house?

BONE DIGGER

1.
This morning Father Martin gave me Gregory's book of Psalms.

At vespers I sit, listening to the monks voices,
a sweetness like pasture sage infuses the air.
Allelujah, hallelujah
praise to God at the gates of Zion.

2.
wascana (oskana): Cree for pile of buffalo bones

3.
Three Brodner brothers now buried in the abbey's graveyard.

What does it take to be a believer?

4.
I would go to visit the bones of my grandparents, over there,
but where? The football field where they dug their own graves?
What perishes and what lasts forever?

Does the earth care where they've vanished?
Prairie dust blows here, the earth's dry as bone,
their dust is now wind, wind in my hair.

5.
Every white person here from pulled-up roots, kept moist
for the journey, by foot, in ox carts, carriages, stinking bellies of ships,
days and nights on wooden benches of trains,
     the end of the line a bleached grass sea
and vaster sky – in daylight and starlight – heaven's theatre

(. . . *the glory of God, the firmament tells His handiwork* –)

ten thousand repetitions, echo after echo,
replanted, the like with the like, the grid already sketched out
on blank paper, each inch a mile of latitude and longitude,
hungry to fill each space with names.

6.
wascana (oscana): *a great tragedy happened here*

7.
Evening walk, no cars, crunching gravel on the road,
I close my eyes, the sun glowing amber inside my eyelids,
each footstep a song of praise, a plain song, a fluttering joy,
the wheat fields, waving, the barley whispering,
birdsong another sweetness, the song unknown,
until I find myself on the road's left shoulder
beside blanket flowers and blue beardtongues,
bringing home specimens to learn their names.

8.

Milosz says *only the moment is eternal;*
for this, here, gratitude, relief
from the weight of record, the need
to capture each moment in a fine mesh net,
                                        rinse
then string into words, scratch onto pages.

A DAUGHTER RECOGNIZES A FATHER WHO SPOKE

for Paul Celan from Czernowitz, Bukovina

I see you

writing your Jew-heart
with the executioners' pen,
carving words snatched
from *a thousand darknesses.*

My own father's heart
a private honeycomb
kept out of sight,
entombed

      after *that which happened,* your choices.

I read your heart's inscriptions:

mandel-eyed mother scar,
barbed-wire father scar, whose hand you let go,
heart scar a perfect globe
complete

like the tattooed man I saw
in a book of inspiration,
every skin surface needled with pigment,
an ocean, fish, waves. Shirtless, a living poster:
I am beauty made flesh, the tattooed
one announced.

Yiddish in North America

Is it really my fault if by error
sheyn happens to rhyme with geveyn?
That longing, genuine longing
is always alone with its pain?

— Itzik Manger

O language of my cradlesongs,
breath of my parents' loss,
sweet cry from the burnt over-there,
beckoning call from the *grine* clubhouse,
tongue of our difference

O graceful script of quill and black ink
your letters identical to the holy ones,
but shameless double agent,
pick up artist of the local lingo,
cleverest fool, you
couldn't foresee your disappearance
from just about every Jewish home

Despised old-country survivor,
clobbered by Hebrew's upper hand,
the return to Zion your worst extinguishment.
I count on the salty-tears of you,
to prod my heavy tongue awake,
yearn for the sound of your tremble-throated song,
last remnant of the ember-world

Now you're a seasoning for our fusion table,
found in every good cook's cupboard,
zaltz un fefer to sprinkle in the soup,

your fridge-magnet words amusement
for kitchen poets, while your
libraries have been packed up,
shipped to Massachusetts, your faded
script from ledgers and tombstones
saved in an archive in Winnipeg, soon to be closed.

I'm in the kitchen, wiping my eyes, listening as you sing.

Finding Kutz

SURPRISE GIFT

In the company of writers, in the mountains of Alberta,
I met a woman seeking her past. She offered me a story
and two photographs: her Jewish grandfather and Lena,
his Jewish wife, came as settlers to Saskatchewan.

Lena died in childbirth. He was grateful to leave his daughter in
the care of Métis women who came to help. He moved away,
remarried, and took his Jewish secret to his grave.

A kaddish for Lena and her family.

Lena's Kaddish

1. *Postkarte*

Lena's framed by marguerites,
their petals tied by black ribbons
as she floats inside the frame,
almond face in soft shadow,
sweep of gleaming hair pure Klimt.
Her eyes are lit with light that mourns
her stillborn child, but believes
in second chances.

In her ruffled lace collar,
her photo, her *gedenken*
a dopisnice, a carte universelle:

> "It's night, but our ship is lit by a rose moon.
> Soon, the other end of the world . . ."

2. Winter Birth

Look closely, and you'll see me,
a man swallowed by the shadow
of our *pitsele* cabin, so small
my head is level with its crown
of snow.

I've had no way to tell you what happened there,
but you deserve to know.

The birth ripped my heart in two.
Forgive me, then I understood the prayer
thanking *got* I was not born
a woman.

After, I could rejoice, but just
for a moment.

Lena's fever grew only hotter, as
I ran wild, boiling chokecherry tea,
but couldn't stop the bleeding,
the entire bed a crimson sea.

If I'd been a horse,
I could have saved her,
galloped to Prince Albert
for the doctor,
but I was the drift caught in the branches
holding my broken sparrow, *my kleyninke,*
in the blue curve of sorrow.

3. *Métis Ni-mamasak*

      Holding my broken sparrow, my *kleyninke,*
      in the blue curve of sorrow,

three Métis women appeared
at my cabin door.

Death, our common language,
pulled them across the beaten snow,
tuned their ears to the cries of my *kleyninke,*
her rosebud mouth seeking breast
but finding only shadow

until their shadows squeezed the walls
of our aching home.

        we shall feed her the milk of the forest,
        the song of the hidden river,
        and when the sun's heat
        has brought the snowmelt,
        she will return to you, an alpine flower,
        a primrose, a dark-throated shooting star.

What choice had I, but to let her go?

METISSAGE

a weaving,
French and Cree
a blood mixing
Michif a language
a pile of buffalo bones
arrowpoint and feather
beaded flowers
adorning skins
sewn into jackets,
gloves with fringes
sticks and stones
strips of land
cut up from a river
the stook of settlement
the map no longer true
the warp and weft unraveled
the notes disappeared,
no directions to guide
tongue and lip-smack,
rouse the inner-ear snails
with memories of prairie
cradlesong
say metissage
say tissage
say sage
say

       say

Driving Through Bienfait Saskatchewan

Why not consider the fate of beans? Does the prairie care
what names are pinned to its mounds and curves and waters?
Imports all, the beans and their planters, supplanters of the
mixed up and metissaged.

French nouns and Cree verbs bounced in this wind,
in Michif, a hybrid language – like Yiddish, I'm told.

The sounds of Michif blown away, as the Métis were blown,
by the whistle of locomotives and babble of their cargoes –
Ukranians, Poles, Lithuanians, Latvians, Germans, Romanians,
Hungarians, Czechs, Slovaks, Croatians, Finns, Swedes, Dutch,
French and English. Yiddish, too, stepped off the trains, to claim
a mound, a curve, a little water. A comfort, these familiar sounds,
in such strange surroundings?

Just like astronomers discovering distant stars, or botanists
who lend their names to the fruit of their genetic manipulations,
the railway funders also were rewarded. Monsieur Bienfait from
Paris, successful stock-seller for the CPR, a toast to your
posthumous honorific! Well done!

It's a small town, still, where beans do grow, but the season
is short. The sounds of Michif, like Yiddish, may be trapped
in its stones, but night, or day, its sky remains unparalleled.

WAPELLA CEMETERY

We are driving from Rocanville,
we have directions, from the R.M. office,
note the mark in the section showing cemetery,
    yes, it's in a farmer's field,
      seven sections west, two and a half south
      just count each section as a mile, you know
it's tricky in kilometres, counting sections,
on unmarked gravel roads,
    is this a section road or a driveway up a field?

We keep driving, to Wapella's town office,
    but sorry, don't know anything about a Jewish cemetery,
    try Mrs. Surridge, she would know. Nobody home?
    Better go to Moosomin, they'll have all the maps
    you're looking for. Just ask for Heather.

We're raising dust, windows closed,
our piece of section map circled on McCutcheon's field.
We are counting,
    slow down this looks like it might be

we pull into a farmer's drive, with luck,
he knows just what we're looking for,
we're very close,
    now listen, go back out, turn right about a mile,
    on the east side of the road, in the middle of a hayfield,
    you'll see some trees and bushes, some concrete posts.

We pull over where he's sent us,
pass giant rounds of hay, in field freshly stubbled,
arrive at concrete posts, climb through the wire
                              gingerly,
parting tangled mats of grass, thistles as tall as our hips
in search of a sign for ancestral bones,

but this little plot, no larger than a living room,
reveals nothing more than what it grows,
a living monument to fleabane and goat's beard
a stopping place for dragonflies.

A Photograph of Mr. & Mrs. Solomon Barish in Rocanville, 1936

In their living room,
with its tiled fireplace and classical columns,
he's still in his work boots,
she's in her nightcap, all in white.
The end of a long day on Barish farm.
They've prospered since 1895,
living miracles of Jewish enterprise.

Behind her a portrait of Herzl
(the modern Moses who dreamed of Zion)
honoured on the Prairie of Saskatchewan.
His vision, after Dreyfus, couldn't be clearer –
no hope for the Jews in Europe,
only back to the homestead,
where one wall of the holy Temple still stood,
a phantom house calling for restoration,
calling and calling for two thousand years.

But the other Moses, the Baron,
Maurice de Hirsch, is not in this picture.
While Herzl dreamed, the Baron gave rescue –
to Canada, America, Argentina.

Mr. & Mrs. Solomon Barish, in the evening
of their lives, dreaming of Zion
by the Calling River.

In Hirsch

Past avenues of nettles,

where hens once pecked in the yards,

we picked our way

by empty barns, tumbled houses,

searching for the old synagogue

recycled as someone's home.

Past broken windows reeking abandonment,

a sudden vision of my mother's fabled

Pohorolowka, circa 1919,

the year her father bought the flour mill,

she's a child of two

running *borves* in the yard,

oblivious to the muck and rocks beneath her feet,

feet that sang, a capella.

IN HIRSCH'S GRAVEYARD

In Hirsch's graveyard
too many young ones lie
under stones like trees
with their branches shorn,
brief stories of unwed sons and
maiden daughters,
while nearby, aspens call

In Hirsch's graveyard
blessed thanks to the Baron
and to the Baroness,
for the rescue,
for the promise,
for the dollars in the millions
that sustained life
amidst the hardship and the losses

In Hirsch's graveyard
the legacy of humanity
made your heir,
care of your sisters and brothers
carved in every stone
while nearby, aspens call
the meadowlarks home

Finding Kutz in Edenbridge Cemetery

If you could speak, Kutzele,
I'd ask where you came from.
Who knows, we may be related.

My great-*Bubbe* Sarah
was a Kutz from Berezne.
You don't know Berezne?
Near Rovne, once Poland,
now the Ukraine. There may be
a Vilna connection –
weren't many of you Litvaks?
You see, it's possible.

Perhaps you knew her, she
married a Kramer, and
I see Cramer here, too.
Is this coincidence?
We know those scribes, when you
got off the boat, asked your name,
then wrote what they pleased.
A *C* or a *K,* to them,
what's the difference?

So Kutzele, tell me,
what brought you to the *pardes*
of Eden? I've looked on the
map I picked up in Brooksby,
with all the homesteaders,
a name in each square, but yours,
I can't find. So Kutzele,
what's the story?

Wouldn't it be something if
there's something between us?
I'm asked all the time what's
my Saskatchewan con-
nection. None, to be honest,
except ten days in Lumsden,
with a visit to Lipton.

These days they say if it's not
your story, you shouldn't
write it. Like you're trespassing.

But a Yid is a Yid,
we are all scattered seeds,
and the tree grows within
us, however it's named.

You should have heard me,
the prairie *grine* −
what's this tree, an aspen?
a poplar? with shimmering
leaves that sound like rain,
and the *feygelekh,*
where's my bird book?
and countless wildflowers
edging the fields −
this is oat? or is it barley?
such a *nudnik* − every minute,
stop the car please, I've got
to take another picture.

But in the graveyard, I shone,
knowing Hebrew, and many
thanks for my surprise today,
when I looked at the photo
I took of your grave. So *Kutz*
could be *Katz,* you're a *Cohen!*
and me, a *bas Cohen* –
my father, *zikhrono l'brokha.*

I get excited to find
mishpokha. We have so
little, as you know.
It must have been agony
wondering what happened
to those, like us, who were left
behind. What about your brothers
and sisters, aunts and uncles,
nieces and nephews, all your friends?

Thanks for building that
beautiful *shul.* Yes, it's still
standing, a living museum
with no lock on its door,
filled with such *ruakh,*
the sweetness of warm aged wood.

Entering was like stepping
into a tree, with the light
of the sky tinted green from
the fields, flowing in, like
the river down the gravel
road, where you named your bridge.

Of course I took pictures,
and in my favourite,
out of inky water,
an iridescent blue,
cloud-flecked sky.

A young man I met in
Winnipeg, whose *Bubbe*
you probably knew, dreamed
of having his *khupah* there,
but the wedding party
didn't want to travel
so far, with no catering,
hotels, or bars around.

Sol's *Bubbe* told me
her parents never wanted
to leave, they'd worked hard
creating their simple
paradise, needed nothing
more. But the *kinder* didn't stay –
education, marriage,
everything they wanted
was somewhere away.

I've got to give you a
yasher koakh, for living
eighty-seven years – no small
feat, for someone born
in 1877,
who crossed half the world
surprised himself and everyone,
to become a Jewish farmer
in Northern Saskatchewan.

A Few Words about Reading
Mike Usiskin's Edenbridge Memoir,

Oxen un motorin, in Yiddish, every evening for a week while
I visited my mother last summer, from an original copy that
came from Winnipeg's Yiddish library that's now in Aaron
Lansky's Yiddish Book Centre in Massachusetts. It tells of
Mike leaving Russia as a young man in 1906, for London,
then Saskatchewan, a few years later. His memoir reveals the
wonder and horror of life in the bush. He's heartbreaking and
hilarious. A friend allowed me to borrow this treasure, so I was
able to follow along with the English version I picked up at the
Jewish Archives in Winnipeg translated by Mike's niece, which
was a good thing, because mother did most of the reading, hardly
giving me the chance, she was just too hungry to read Yiddish
after so many years of not, plus she had no patience for my
plodding, as slow as Mike's two-day *farblondzhete* trek through
the mud to get from his soddy to the post office – another
farblotikte shack. Yes mother got a big kick out of Edenbridge,
and loved that the name was a play on *Yiden* which is
pronounced *Yeeden* so drop the Y and get Eden why not?
They needed a name when they got the bridge so Jews
in Paradise made her laugh and Mike was so dear,
mogere keshenes and all.

MIKE USISKIN AS RECALLED BY GABRIELLE ROY

in her memoir *The Fragile Light of Earth* she remembers

*him pushing aside his books and the scraps of paper that he had
ruffled on the table in a dreamlike way. He came to see us off at the
gate, which had been made from a barn door, with a little opening in
the lower part so that his cat could go in and out at will. The master
of the house bent down to help a larkspur which had been knocked
over by the rain. When I turned back for the last time, I saw more
clearly than on arriving how miserable was this threshold in the midst
of the forest, and how solitary this man whose hands sought the
company of flowers. And yet it seemed to me then and still does
today, that this poor colonist had achieved a level of happiness that
thousands like him had searched for since God knows how long*

Lipton Hebrew Cemetery
Second Visit

Mendele,
It's the little padlocked door on the back of your grave house
that puzzles me.

Could you not bear to be cooped up for long?

Maybe Meyerovitch took that into account,
when he built your little *shteebl*
in the row *bayim fentz,* with the other boys,
    young Mendele, he said to himself, *this boy needs*
    to get out from time to time,
    to roam a little . . .

No front door on your grave house, but
a plain tin plate, echoing a schoolboy's cutout
of a house, complete with roof,
announcing in faded Hebrew script,
your name, your father's,
and the date of your death, in *Shevat,*
the coldest month of winter.

Could it have been a spooked horse
in a sneaky blizzard, pouncing
as you drove the wagon filled with wood?
Only eleven, but already your back sturdy as a hasp, defiant,
wind biting at your flesh

or was it illness swooped into you,
that no remedy, not even poison bluestone could dislodge?

(a miracle, Frau Silverman, but great caution required:
dissolve in a glass of warm water, just enough to colour it.
Dip a feather in the solution, paint his throat.)

I want to know who remembers you with *kaddish?*
Who comes with the padlock's key?

Mrs. W Speaks from Her Suicide Grave House

I hate the slick vinyl siding, the new green roof.

A bloody mess I made, to haunt
my husband's every night,
as each night my bones were chewed
and spit out by the cold.
Every morning I woke to
more strewn around my bed,
my leg bones, my backbones,
their dainty hollows wells of darkness,
my finger bones, ivory needles.
In the end, I had no water to draw,
no cloth to stitch.
All I wanted was to be warm.

How they hurried, burning straw
far into night, to heat the earth enough
to accept a shovel, while I laughed so hard,

as I was already frozen, a golem
made of sod, without heartbeat,
long before I lay in that black
sarcophagus for my final bath.
I turned the water scarlet,
like Moses before Pharoah,
let me go, let me go, I pleaded,
but my master was deaf to me

was always in another kingdom, seeking
a sack of flour, a few potatoes,
some wood for the oven,
but even the smell of *challeh* baking
couldn't raise one molecule
of joy in me.

They argued over what to do with me,
planted me as if I were a plague, but
honestly, what did I care?
In the furthest corner of the graveyard,
my rotten house spoke for me.
My *Song of Songs.*

POEM FOR LIL

Lil Schacter, early resident of Lipton
1907–2006

If I could, I'd write
a Yiddish poem for Lil,
for her *yiddishe neshume*
that first saw light
on another kind of promised land,
immigrant land,
cleared of its buffalo,
           (and its buffalo people cleared from view)
a shelterless land,
a land of sky that had no end,
a dark earth mud-house land,
a plow and oxen land,
buffaloberries and saskatoons,
a Swainson's hawk and coyote land
a coldest of the cold cold land
a land of burning

sun. A *Tiferes Yisroel* land,
where Torah freely breathed
amongst aspen and poplar,
and children learned *aleph-bes*
along with *a-b-c*

a hundred years ago, yet
I can only write about the end,
and imagine the beginning,
as Lil's soul returns
to *reboyne-sheloylem,*
with thanks for such a life I've seen,
I hear her saying.

Her eyes, now prairie sky.

CIRCLE BACK THE OTHER WAY: SQUARE DANCE JAMBOREE

The bird in the cage you close the door
The bird hop out the crow hop in

All promenade the floor

Calling River Man, *chasser, chasser*
Swing your partner, dos a dos

Mrs. W. and young Mendele,
face your corners

Tap your heel and save your toes
Lady go on and little boy follow

Onto the next and circle four

Father Martin wrote a letter
How's your mother *Do-si-do*

Lena and *tanis* Marguerite,
The *minyan* from the forest

Métis *ni-mamasak* all,
The Brodner Brothers from St. Pete's,

Tuck away Anne Frank's photo
Grand chain round the hall

Bernadette and Paul Celan,
Swing that gal don't let her fall

Daddy and the German Officer,
Come across the bridge and bow

The Hoffers and the Feldmans,
The sisters Lil and Claire,
Kutzele and the Vickars,
All join hands and circle

Promenade the floor

The bird in the cage you close the door

Gabrielle Roy and Mike Usiskin,
Two days trudging through the bush

Allemande left your corners
Forward and back like a shooting star

Monsieur Bienfait, *chasser* up the river,
Steal that lady like honey from a bee
While the roosters crow and the *feygelekh* sing
Spread out pretty like a three leaf clover

John A. Macdonald and Lord Rothschild,
Alexander Galt and grandpa Mordechai,

Honour your corners, honour your partners
Swing around as you cross over

Baron de Hirsch and Clara,
Sweet Shirley and Ben Kahan,
Mr and Mrs. Barrish,
Frieda and Hilda's brother Ruby,

All round your right hand lady
Left hand lady like a butterfly

Father Martin swings my mother
They promenade the hall

He says mother's gone to heaven
He says joyous like a bride meets groom

The bird hop out, the crow hop in
The forest *minyan* prays

MOURNER'S KADDISH

MAGNIFIED AND SANCTIFIED
MAY HIS GREAT NAME BE
IN THE WORLD THAT HE CREATED,
AS HE WILLS,
AND MAY HIS KINGDOM COME
IN YOUR LIVES AND IN YOUR DAYS
AND IN THE LIVES OF ALL THE HOUSE OF ISRAEL,
SWIFTLY AND SOON, AND SAY ALL AMEN!

AMEN!
MAY HIS GREAT NAME BE BLESSED
ALWAYS AND FOREVER!

BLESSED
AND PRAISED
AND GLORIFIED
AND RAISED
AND EXALTED
AND HONOURED
AND UPLIFTED
AND LAUDED
BE THE NAME OF THE HOLY ONE
(HE IS BLESSED!)
ABOVE ALL BLESSINGS
AND HYMNS AND PRAISES AND CONSOLATIONS
THAT ARE UTTERED IN THE WORLD,
AND SAY ALL AMEN!

MAY A GREAT PEACE FROM HEAVEN —
AND LIFE! —
BE UPON US AND UPON ALL ISRAEL,
AND SAY ALL AMEN!

MAY HE WHO MAKES PEACE IN HIS HIGH PLACES
MAKE PEACE UPON US AND UPON ALL ISRAEL,
AND SAY ALL AMEN!

GLOSSARY

Transliterating Yiddish has too often been a free-for-all. A valiant effort for standardization of transcription has been spearheaded by the YIVO Institute, a Yiddish language and culture organization now based in New York, and I have done my best to conform to its rules. As an unruly and unschooled Yiddishist, I apologize for any lapses in spelling, not to mention my sometimes idiosyncratic definitions of words and phrases.

a kharpe un a bushe – a disgrace, an embarrassment

adonai elokainu adonai ekhad – the Lord is our God, the Lord is One. First line of the "Shema," the fundamental prayer of Judaism

bani – Romanian currency

bas Cohen – daughter of a Cohen

beysoylem – cemetery

borves – barefoot

Bubbe – grandmother (many variations of this – *Bubby, Bobe, Bobie,* etc.)

carte universelle – postcard

challeh – braided egg bread, usually eaten on Friday night, the start of the Sabbath, and holidays (should be written as *khale,* but I just can't)

coup de foudre – French, bolt of lightning, or love at first sight

dopisnice – Czech, postcard

farblondzhete – lost

farblotikte – dirty

feygelekh – birds

gan eydn – garden of Eden

gedenken – souvenir

geveyn – weeping, tears

gornisht – nothing

grine – greenhorn, newcomer, survivor

gut shabes – "Good Sabbath," traditional greeting

hayeled – Hebrew, the boy

heylikn zeydn – holy, righteous grandfather

khaloshesdik – hideous, ugly

khapper – grabber, kidnapper

khevra kadisha – Jewish
burial society

khupah – marriage canopy

kind – child; *kinder* – children

kleyninke – little one

meydele – little girl

mameloshn – mother tongue

mandel – almond

me darf hob'n rakhmones –
you've got to have pity

mes – dead person, corpse

minyan – a group of ten
Jews; required number
to say Kaddish

mishpokha – family

mogen david – Star of David,
six-pointed Jewish star

mogere keshines – lean
or nearly empty pockets

nign – a melody

ni-mamasak – Michif, mothers

nudnik – a pain in the neck

olam haba – the next
world, eternity, the afterlife

olam hazeh – this world,
life on earth

pardes – paradise

pitsele – a tiny or little one

pletzel – a flat, baked
bun topped with onions

reboyne-sheloylam – Master
of the Universe, a term
of endearment for God

ruakh – spirit, from
the Hebrew

sha shtil – be quiet

shekhina – God's female
presence

shema yisroel – "Hear O Israel,"
opening words of the funda-
mental prayer of Judaism

Shevat – a month in the
Hebrew calendar, correspon-
ding to January or February

sheyn – beautiful

shiva – seven day period
of observance following
loved one's death

shmire – sitting with,
literally guarding the body
of a deceased between death
and burial

shney – snow

shul – synagogue

shvuos – holiday celebrating
the giving of the Torah in
Sinai, falling around June,
the beginning of summer

shtetl – village or the Jewish
section of a village in Eastern
Europe

shtikl broyt – a little
piece of bread

sukke – a booth, temporary
structure with roof of branches
and leaves, commemorating the
Harvest Festival, *Sukkot,* and 40
years of wandering in the
desert. Falls around September

tallis – a prayer shawl

tanis – Michif, baby

tiferes yisroel – "The Glory
of Israel"; often the name
of a synagogue or school

tsezeyt un tseshpreyt – sown to
the wind, scattered, dispersed

vaybele – little wife

yasher koakh –
congratulations for
an honour or accomplishment

yiddishe neshume – Jewish soul

yisgadal v'yiskadash –
Hebrew/Yiddish; magnified
and sanctified, first words
of the Mourner's Kaddish

yortsayt – anniversary
of the death of a loved one

zikhrono l'brokha – may
his memory be a blessing

zmire – a song, or melody,
often in praise of Sabbath

Notes and Credits

Many of the poems and prose pieces are based upon personal interviews, original documents, memoirs, journals and books. Notes refer to the sources of the material presented, or that inspired the work.

Frontispiece: Yiddish map of Canada, from Abraham Rhinewine's *Kanade, Geshikhte un Entviklung,* Farlag Pulishers, Toronto, 1923. With thanks to the Jewish Public Library, Montreal, QC

Photo of Lipton Hebrew Cemetery: Isa Milman, 2003

Grave House
Robert Pogue Harrison, *The Dominion of the Dead,* University of Chicago Press, 2003

David G. Mandelbaum, *The Plains Cree: an ethnographic, historical and comparative study,* Canadian Plains Studies, University of Regina, 1936

Insert of Lipton in Mandelbaum's map: produced by mapmaker Todd Golumbia, 2007

Photograph, Indian Cemetery (Cree), Fort Qu'Appelle, SK, May 1885, by Otto B. Buell, National Archives of Canada, PA118766, Ottawa, ON

After 1881, the Year of the Tzar's Assassination
Erna Paris, *Jews: An Account of their Experience in Canada,* McMillan 1980 "*Ole Clo,*" slang term for Jew, deriving from the peddler's call of "old clothes"; Lord Rothschild never did respond to Alexander Galt's request for funding

A Few Restrictions Regarding the Jews of Romania,
1885–1900; Fusgeyers, 1900
Jill Culinar, *Finding Home: In the Footsteps of the Jewish Fusgeyers,*
Sumach Press, 2004

The Forest Prays
From a passage in Jacob Baltzan's *Memoirs of a Pioneer Farmer in
Western Canada at the Dawn of the Twentieth Century,* assembled
from a series of his articles published in 1936–1937 in the Israelite
Press, Winnipeg, MB

Jewish Settlers' F.A.Q.s
From a pamphlet produced by the Jewish Colonization
Association, Winnipeg, MB circa 1912; Archives, Jewish Heritage
Centre of Western Canada, Winnipeg, MB

A Pioneer Girl's Diary: July 1887
Maryanne Caswell, *Pioneer Girl,* McGraw Hill, 1964

Plan of Township 22
Archives, Jewish Heritage Centre of Western Canada, John
Reichman collection, JHC490, Winnipeg, MB

A Thing of Beauty Cut from Ash
Inspired by tools from Golumbia's "Prosperity Farm," Macrorie,
SK and conversations with Todd, Joe and Arnold Golumbia

Red Harvest
Inspired by conversations with Ben Kahan, last Jewish farmer
from Lipton, SK

Manager Baker Explains the Causes of Discontent
Among Settlers
Unidentified newspaper story, from Archives, Jewish Heritage
Centre, Winnipeg, MB

MAGGIE WASSERMAN BROWNSTONE'S DIARY entry noted in
Erna Paris' *Jews: An Account of their Experience in Canada,* 1980

A PAGE FROM A LIPTON LEDGER
Archives, Jewish Heritage Centre of Western Canada, JHC520,
Winnipeg, MB

LETTER FROM WM J. CRUTCHFIELD, Archives, Jewish Heritage
Centre, Winnipeg, MB

ADVICE FROM A GRANDFATHER
From Cherie Smith, *Mendel's Children: A Family Chronicle,*
Calgary, University of Calgary Press, 1997

WHEN THE GRASS FIRST FELT THE PLOUGH
Title and inspiration from Trevor Herriot, *River in a Dry Land: A
Prairie Passage,* Toronto, Stoddart, 2000

HUSBANDRY
Inspired by conversations with Anna Feldman, in remembrance
of Branche Feldman

MY MOTHER'S *Sukkele* SONG
Sabina Kramer Milman, recorded by Sheldon Pollock, Cape Cod,
1978

BRIDGES
Reb Nachman of Bratzslav, 18th century Hassidic sage

AMBER RASPBERRIES
The book about the Jews is *Land of Hope* by Clara Hoffer & F.H.
Kahan, Modern Press, Saskatoon, 1960

BONE DIGGER
a great tragedy happened here – a reversal of the Chanukah *dreydl*
acronym, remembering that *a great miracle happened there* – Jewish
victory over Hellenist oppression in the land of Israel

A DAUGHTER RECOGNIZES A FATHER WHO SPOKE
Inspired by John Felstiner's *Paul Celan: Poet, Survivor, Jew,* Yale
University Press, 1995

SURPRISE GIFT; LENA'S KADDISH
Series is based on family stories and photos belonging to
Melanie Dugan, with thanks

WAPELLA CEMETERY
The R.M. stands for Rural Municipality office, where property
and other records are kept; the cemetery boundaries are pre-
served by Mr. McCutcheon, who owns and farms the field con-
taining the cemetery

MR. & MRS. SOLOMON BARISH DREAMING OF ZION IN
ROCANVILLE, 1936
From a photograph seen in various sources, including Cyril Edel
Leonoff's *The Architecture of Jewish Settlements in the Prairies: A
Pictorial History,* Jewish Historical Society of Western Canada, 1975

FINDING KUTZ IN EDENBRIDGE CEMETERY
From conversations with Sol Nagler, Hilda Springman, Freeda
Baron, Norm Vickar

A FEW WORDS ABOUT READING MIKE USISKIN'S
EDENBRIDGE MEMOIR
Uncle Mike's Edenbridge, translated by Marcia Usiskin Basman,
Peguis Publishers, Winnipeg, 1983
Gabrielle Roy, *The Fragile Light of Earth,* translated by Alan
Brown, McClelland & Stewart, 1982 (original *Fragiles lumieres de
la terre,* 1978)

CIRCLE BACK THE OTHER WAY: SQUARE DANCE JAMBOREE
Richard Kraus, *Square Dances of Today and How to Teach and Call Them,* Barnes & Co., 1950; Gene Gowing, *The Square Dancers' Guide,* and the CD *Square Dancing Made Easy (with calls by Slim Jackson)* tuned my ears to the dance; many thanks to Don McKay for the idea

MOURNER'S KADDISH
Translation by Leon Wieseltier, *Kaddish,* Vintage Books, 1998

ACKNOWLEDGEMENTS

From the day I first stood in Lipton's Hebrew Cemetery, this labour of love was crafted with the help of many. To all, I extend my heartfelt gratitude. To Linda Doctoroff, for planting the first seed. To Diane Buchanan, for enthusiastically joining me on an outing to Lipton, and for asking the questions that set me on the journey.

Thanks to Lil Schacter, Claire Shaffer, Anna Feldman, Gladys Rose, Freeda Baron, Sol Nagler, Hilda Springman, Norm Vickar, Little Vickar, Melanie Dugan, Linda Ghan, Ben Kahan, Sydney and Bob Kalef, the Golumbias: Joe, Colleen, Todd, Patty and Arnold, Beverlea Sinclair, Sandy and Naomi Horodesky, and others whose names I failed to record, for sharing your family stories. I couldn't be more blessed.

Enormous gratitude to Irma Penn and staff at the Jewish Heritage Centre in Winnipeg, whose passion and knowledge brought forth documents that I thought only existed in my dreams – documents from which this book took form.

Thanks to Hilary Craig for taking off with a stranger for a four thousand kilometre pilgrimage, with atlases, maps, bird and plant books and good cheer; Joyce & Allan Hoge, Bernadette Wagner, Dave Margoshes, the Beth Jacob synagogue of Regina, St. Peter's Monastery in Muenster, and Father Martin Brodner, my especially dear friend, whose soul is now in heaven. Thanks to Rabbi Harry Brechner and Lynn Greenough, for discussions about Jewish burial practices and beliefs. Thanks to David Kaetz for Yiddish conversation and the loan of *Oxen un motorin,* and to Goldie Morgentaler for skillfully polishing the rust off my Yiddish, and making it sparkle. Ditto to Greg Schofield for checking the Michif/Cree.

Thanks to the Canada Council for the Arts for believing in my project, and to the Victoria Epilepsy & Parkinson's Centre for releasing me for six months to work on it; thanks to the BC Arts Council, and to the Banff Centre for the Arts for a blissful five weeks of supported writing, and to my brilliant mentors Don McKay, Tim Bowling and Anne Simpson, who lit my path the many times I was lost in the forest. Special thanks to Diane Douglas, for her close reading and inspired editorial suggestions, and to all my writing studio mates for rooting me on. Wendy Morton, Arleen Pare, Heidi Garnett, Jeanette Lynes for critical reading and suggestions, and Betsy Warland for early assistance in shaping the book. Thanks to Lorna Crozier for advice from a native daughter, and to Patrick Lane for Glenairley retreats where poetry wisdom flowed into these pages.

And always, thanks to Robert McConnell for unfailingly offering his ear, eye and heart, and for feeding me exquisitely.

And for eternity, to my beloved mother, in *olam habah,* whose life illuminates these pages, and whose memory shall always be for a blessing.

Victoria, September 2007

ABOUT THE AUTHOR

*I*sa Milman is a poet, visual artist and occupational therapist who has lived in Canada for the past 30 years. Her first poetry collection, *Between the Doorposts,* won the 2005 Poetry Prize at the Canadian Jewish Book Awards. She has also published a chapbook, *Seven Fat Years,* and her work has appeared in a number of journals and anthologies.

A daughter of Holocaust survivors, Isa Milman was born in a displaced persons camp in Germany before immigrating to Boston. She graduated from Tufts University, then lived in San Francisco and Paris, involving herself in improvisational dance and theatre activities. She obtained her masters degree in rehabilitation science, and secured a job teaching occupational therapy at McGill University. She currently works as a program coordinator at the Victoria Epilepsy and Parkinson's Centre.